Common Wealth
A Sequence

Common Wealth
A Sequence

David Donaldson

Matador
9 Priory Business Park,
Wistow Road, Kibworth Beauchamp,
Leicestershire. LE8 0RX
Tel: 0116 279 2299
Email: books@troubador.co.uk
Web: www.troubador.co.uk/matador
Twitter: @matadorbooks

ISBN 978 1838594 091

British Library Cataloguing in Publication Data.
A catalogue record for this book is available from the British Library.

Printed and bound in Great Britain by 4edge Limited
Typeset in 12pt Baskerville by Troubador Publishing Ltd, Leicester, UK

Matador is an imprint of Troubador Publishing Ltd

Contents

This England...

This raft of rock;
this precious fragment of welling magma,
heaved out of equatorial seas in the world's youth;

this plug wrenched out of Pluto's realm
to sear the atmosphere with fire and buckle up
to the heights of the Himalayas, Helvellyn, Snowdon;

this lava desert, this seat of fire cooking
beneath sulphur skies, substance of tectonic quarrels
in the slow-drifting deeps of time...

*

this limestone repository of warm primordial seas,
dark-laden with memorials of steaming forests
and lumbering lizard horrors...folded, folded...

wrapped once more in the cool winding sheet of the sea
receiving to its compacted core the cast-off shells
of myriads settling on the ocean floor like steady rain...

*

this buried image of what-is-to-be
arising with the shuddering Alps, raising
rough-cast shoulders of chalk to a changed sky;
to suddenly familiar grasses, birds and beasts;

this heavenly hell of volcanic fire,
rumbling raft of life cooling, past its prime,
scoured clear with ice, its pride of peaks vanished

to strew the fertile plains, its fiery furnaces
burnt out- and alight in the bowels of long-toothed predators...

*

this crumpled cemetery of shell and bone
embalmed in grave depths of sea and earth,
this island cast adrift by the melting snows;

this wildwood of oak and birch,
this wilderness of wolves and trackless wastes,
marsh and deep mirroring pools where curlew and bittern
    call...

*

this land of Men,
of the chambered tomb, the stone circle, the upland dead;
this tribal outpost of imperial Rome; this land

of the holy thorn, of monks and monasteries, burghs
and thegns, of fervent knights on mystic quests,
of coasts alight and homesteads razed;

this property of the King, this province of the Pope,
this Eden of pristine wastes, drained swamps,
of common land and hamlets hidden in labyrinths of lanes

where brambles and roses contend in the wild hedgerows...

*

this land of arch and spire, of sacred shrines
and pilgrim ways, of pilaged monasteries,
martyrs burning at the stake, axe and block
to sever heads and the divine right of kings;

this realm of dauntless spirits circling the globe,
of roaming beggars and vagabonds, the hangman's
public noose; this land of open commons,
patchwork fields fenced and hedged,

of smoking cities, mercantile monopolies,
its peasantry displaced; this land
of ancient sunlight harnassed to imperial sway,
of iron machines and rails forged in the white heat

of furnace fires; this drumming heart of empire
on which the sun has set, hellish heaven
of motorways and shopping malls, fire-powered,
fossil-fuelled, display of plenty, of awakened power...

this store of legends and laboratories, this realm
of the holy grail, of the atom split in two, of the book
of life bound in a double helix opened up to view;

this land of the all-wanting Wounded King,
of Avalon and Arthur-who-will-come-again;
this Jerusalem-that-is-to-be, this Albion,
Blake's giant stretched out still like the treeless hills

asleep... dreaming its humanity a passing episode
in the soulless Life of Things, and stirring to wake?
or dreaming on...
                    dreaming on....?

Blessed
Continuance

Avebury

1

Stranded rockfall from heaven.
Glimpse of an ancient sea,
A lost horizon. Pock-marked

Sarsens shape and weathering
Like a casting of the runes. What
Do they say? What do they say?

Gap-toothed relics in a great
Cracked bowl. The main road
To elsewhere driven through

With no thought of car parks
Filling, filling with the tourist tide,
Folk posing to be photographed.

*

Her-story not His. Yet on the cusp,
Like Jacob, head stone-pillowed

Dreaming

The primordial Unity, the comings
And goings between Earth and Stars.

Avebury

2

Worlds away
From the parked ranks of vehicles,
Metallic alien appearences
On a green plain. It's we

Step out of them, revenants
On home-return,
Sun-bright wakefulness

Casting our long past into obscurity,
Its elusive ghosts spellbound
In stones such as these

And awaiting their release:
Once fluent in the light's script
Inscribed in stone-cast shadows

Star-aligned, and knowing
Long before the restless
Prodigal ventured to leave home

That Earth's well-being
Was our own.

Blessed Continuance

Neolithic Britain

A ringed hilltop. Mythic island
In a flowering wilderness. Plain,
Marsh, forest. Thin streaks of smoke
Drift from the thatch of clustered huts;

Water glints through gaps in the forest canopy
And there's a clearing, the merest
Nibble at the forest's fringe where
Field patterns have been laid out.

Tiny figures are tending crops; others
Watch over herds of sheep and goats.
Their wealth and joy, this pastoral patch
Won with antler pick, flint axe.

A maze of paths join hilltop, fields,
Forest, the plain beyond. The blue
Of heaven's above, the fertile earth
Beneath. What is this if not Paradise

After long ages of ice, or the stark
Tundra their ancestors had to cross
In the far-off days of wandering?
Yet the plain's astir as never before:

A new enclosure, pits dug for planting
Upright, stones that dwarf the figures
Grouped around with ropes and rollers.
The rhythms of the heavens, the ever-

Varying elements, seed time and harvest,
Births, deaths, ancestral mysteries, cry
To the heart-mind from the pulsing blood
For such an all-encompassing response

To guard the Rounds that grant
Their blessed continuance on Earth.

Stoney Littleton
Long Barrow

near Wellow, Somerset

Place of gathering. Womb and tomb.
The entrance open, shadowing chambers
To left and right. I crawl to the far end,
Crouch back against blackness of earth
Or stone, eyes fixed on the entrance,
Its square of light. And pray. That Earth

Be loved and honoured now as then
When 'then' was old even to those
Who raised Stonehenge, let alone
To the Romans, with their new-fangled swords
And dreams of conquest, dreams so much
Rehearsed since then: of dominion,

Power to command the means no matter
What the costs. But when the costs return
To haunt the dreams, like storm clouds
We've ignored until their massed darkness
Bears down so low we're sealed in?
Then, our sun-alignments long let lapse,

What follows is- collapse, a Fall of Rome.
So I pray where we once gathered,
Joined hands (the living and the dead)
For Earth to be loved and honoured
Now as then. And- as if in answer,
The wall behind me thins and falls away

And I'm outside in the sun and air,
Up there in the summer blue with slow-
Circling buzzards and the crazy
Swooping flight of swallows, expanding
From my little point of self, as if I
Were so much more: this other Self,

A source of wealth and health so vast,
The World were held in its embrace.

The Death of Pan

The Garden

Ancient Egypt

No taste of moon-dust where Ra abounds
His sun-boat riding primordial chaos.
His presence saturates the sky reflecting

Off the water, his lotus eye wide open
On the surface of the lake. The garden's
This formal rectangle softened by plants,

Sycomore figs, varieties of palm and vines
Clustering near the water's edge each
The abundance of a ruling Power, each

Gifted Presence ever to be held in eye
And heart and mind. Then- *Hail to thee, Hapi!*
(The garden's watered by a canal drawn

From the overflowing heavens of the Nile).

Set Aside

Ancient Greece

No gardens. Rather, untended groves- the loveliest-
Set aside for the invisible Ones, temples raised
To honour their indwelling. In Homer, every

River's present at a council of the gods, every
Nymph of the springs and groves and meadows,
All the dryads of the trees. It's never we alone

Rejoice in *the blue season of blossom-bearing spring,*
Or in *the delicate dew o*n the light green grass
As hillsides and meadows return to flower.

And who but Dionysus *bringer of grape bunches,*
Inspires us to bind our hair *with clusters
Of flowering ivy?* Whose but His the ecstasy

That makes us sing and dance? Gardens-
What the need? Save, perhaps, for those
Public spaces set aside beneath the shade of trees

Where we meet to catch the dawning rays
        Of Apollo's sunlit thoughts.

The Death of Pan

Ancient Rome

Tiberius is convinced. There before him
Thamus, ship's pilot, a trembling witness
Testifying how they lay becalmed off Palodes

Until he dared to speak the ghostly words
He'd been ordered to repeat as the breezes
Swelled their sails off Paxi. *When you come*

To Palodes, tell them Great Pan is dead, and
Of the horror of the wailing that filled the air
Though not a soul was visible on shore.

There before him, this trembling witness
Home from sea and bearing the oracular news
From subject Greece to the imperial Majesty.

And the Emperor is convinced.

*

Great Pan is dead. But there is topiary.
And slaves. Those *faceless* ones, appointed
Topiarii to shape submissive nature into

Hunting scenes or fleets of ships or letters
Clipped in box to spell the owner's name.
Great Pan is dead. But there's engineering

Will create commemoration of a spirit-past
Even in the absence of a spring: bring water
To a decorative nympheum. Wherever

You walk or stroll there's order, symmetry:
Tree-lined avenues arrow-straight, fences,
Pergolas, sunken lawns. A temple to Hercules.

Pax Romana without- and within the garden wall.

*

The Garden-Sepulchre

Floats over an abyss. Put your ear
To a fissure in the rock, you'll hear,
Far below, the sound of rushing waters,

The earth torn wide, once restless
With billowing steam and fumes
And sudden bursts of flame. In later times

A ravine of Oracles. In his wisdom,
Solomon filled it in. And so it comes
To pass, after a tumult of years,

Of cries and hammering, one subject
To the rule of Rome and put to death
Outside the city wall, is laid to rest

Within a garden-sepulchre nearby.
Throughout the night earth tremors
Shake the old divide, re-open glimpses

Into *Adam's grave*. As dawn breaks,
The tremors die away and a woman
In tears of bewildered grief stands asking

> One she takes to be the gardener,
> 'Where have you taken him?
> Tell me, where has he gone?'

The Christian Good

St Benedict 480 AD – 547AD

Imperial Rome's a receding memory.
Its broken arches, roofless columns,
Littered masonry; the vacant plinths
Of statues melted down, paving

Ripped-up and overgrown. Remains
Never to be made good; memories
Of terror pursued by terror: the breath
Of Atilla, the Vandals' unsparing sword.

*

You're young and here to study. Shocked
As you pick your way through desolate
Public spaces, the squalor of the poor.

And here is where your future's meant
To lie; perhaps rising in the self-serving
Bureaucracy of what survives.

You'll need a good grasp of Rhetoric,
Its powers to persuade irrespective
Of the truth. You look on as friends

Practice lives of easy pleasure,
Squander wealth and their integrity.
And what of your own inheritance?

Your parents' hopes for you (and
The family wealth)? The comfort
Of your country home? And your duty

To serve the Christian good of Rome?

*

You have to get away, the world in ruins,
Its smouldering temptations. It's like fleeing
Contagion, plague; not that you've turned

Hermit. Your old nurse goes along with you.
In Enfide, you're faced with an impasse. Not
To return means forfeiting your inheritance.

Now begins your climb steeper and steeper.
From the known comforts of the valley floor,
You ascend the side of a ravine, searching out

A cave (the womb in which you'll start again).
Sheer above you, on the summit, a monastery;
Far below, glint of a lake, a jewel set amidst

Palace ruins, one of Nero's, a daily sight
To contemplate. Your cave's only ten feet deep
But now is all the world to you, with Romanus

Of the monastery up above, who has given you
Your hermit's habit, helps you out with food
And guides you through your years of solitude.

*

You labour, weed and clear
And till, so Christ may sow.
It seems there's never an end
To what springs back to be

Uprooted. In your bonfire's
Smoke and flames sensual
Visions reassert their claims
But you never hesitate

To clear out what's in the way,
Your heart set on the Gardener
Risen early with the dew
And addressing you by name.

*

Fame. Admiration. Envy. Attempts to tempt
And poison you. As though all you've wrestled
To subdue within assaults you from without.

But you emerge unscathed from your chrysalis
Of solitude, embrace community, accede
To those high-born in Rome who look to you

To make monks not rhetoricians of their sons.
The mountains about Subiaco sprout monasteries;
Green shoots of hospitality, learning, healing,

Husbandry; new boundaries to the world's waste.
They radiate hope, raised on your founding Rule
Of a life shared in common, binding souls together

In daily work, and constant prayer and praise.

Ora et Labora

Pray and labour. Study, meditate, sing
The Offices eight times on one or two
Plain meals a day. No sleeping early,
No sleeping late. No rusty swords.

When the bell rings your sleepyhead
Awake, it's two in the morning; time
To keep watch, hallow the night,
Process to the Choir by candlelight,

While a lantern passes to and fro
Searching out lids that are fluttering
To close. Labour and pray however
Thick-set with thorns. Push back

The forest, drain fen and marshland,
Reclaim the wilderness, till the earth,
Plant crops. Towns will be born
As settlements cluster about your walls.

You're *schools for the service of the Lord;*
Arks launched to steer a course through
Troubled seas. In your wake a new
World will begin to struggle to its feet.

High Matters of State

The felled forest's grown beyond itself
Into branching canopies of stone,
Pillared avenues, waves of arches

Riding east. Christ, the world's
Perpetual flame, risen to new life
On wings of faith, is *Victor, King*

And *Emperor.* Prayer's a high matter
Of state; life-line to the Divine
Maintained throughout the land

In abbey, church, cathedral:
Perpetual investments in
The eternal Good, state cohesion,

Public-private registration
In the Book of Life. Kings' treasure,
Landed wealth of lords pressed

Into the safe-keeping of those
Possessing nothing save their solemn
Vows to lives of poverty and sacrifice.

The Flowery Mead

The enclosed garden 12th-14th century

A stone wall or wattle fence encloses
A meadow paradise; a studied wilderness
Embroided like a tapestry with violet,
Columbine, lily, rose, with herbs
And fruiting trees. Who wanders here

Builds cathedrals of heart and mind
Now Mary's risen to embrace the heavens.
Birds, trees are the airy flowing
Of her mantle; the flowers trace
Her footsteps over the earth; Natura,

Mother of Creation resurrected
As the bride of Christ. Sit with your beloved
On the turf seat before the ceaseless flowing
Of the spring or fountain of clear water.
As you gaze into each other's eyes,

The constellations come alive.

At the Cutting Edge

The corporate monastery. Prayer, pilgrimage, relics,
All gainful enterprises; guilt's commodified: competing
Offers to remit your sins, time-scales specified; Masses

Chanted for the souls of the donor-dead. Short-falls
In income raised by gambling on the future sales
Of the estate. Sheep to cultivate the landscape;

For the poor displaced, the future beckons: labour
In newly-opened mines, or blast furnaces to tend.
Landlord-abbots prey on tenants; remove those

Who can't pay. Tithes, taxes oppress towns to which
An abbey's given birth; grievances break out in riots;
The corporate monastery. Reviled then as now.

The West's foreshadowing.
                    The fat monk full-fed
                              on too much of a good thing,

The World Reissued

Early Renaissance Garden

A new world's cast off on a rising tide
Of monied wealth. Merchants, bankers
Are aboard with the ruling families.
The library of San Marco's a scholar's
Laboratory for recovering the gold

Of ancient texts. The world's re-issued
In perspective. Subject becomes object.
Natura's set apart, displaced beyond
The vanishing point, her tapestry once
More lapsed into disordered wilderness.

The garden's returned to the architect:
An extension of the house in symmetry
And straight lines. Covered walkways,
Fountains, terraces declare an ordered calm.
Hercules reappears in gigantic statuary.

The garden testifies to its owner's wealth
Of learning and his civilised dignity.

Legendary Magnificence

Villa D'Este 1560-75

The wind's set fair. The Cardinal's
Arrived at the Hesperides. Ladon's
Hundred heads and a dozen law suits
Notwithstanding, the Golden Apples
Are within his reach, hillside and valley
Transformed into a storied world
Of garden rooms. Rome celebrated

And eclipsed. Visitors, ascending
From the valley floor, view with awe
The Herculean Labours on display;
The countless cascades and waterfalls,
The ceaseless play of water jets
In sound and spray; a Water Organ
Babbling madrigals…The stage is set

For fireworks. The hilltop villa (once
A convent) converted as completely
As the hillside, from any backward
Sliding towards Franciscan thoughts.
At every turn each terraced level
Is themed to entertain, instruct,
Amaze; the ruling family embroided

Into tales of its mythological descent.
Here, simple dignity must defer
To legendary magnificence.
Meanwhile, in the lower garden,
Natura takes Her place in the new order:
One more fountain feature spouting
Water from Her many breasts.

World Wonder

Hermetic garden, Heidelberg 1614-19
and the outbreak of the Thirty Years War

Prospero's brave new world is headed
For Heidelberg. Thames is to unite

With Rhine; Elizabeth of England
With Frederick, Lion of the Palatine.

Art, science, religion, the recovered
Wisdom of antiquity's fresh-minted:

Gold of an enlightened alchemy.
Beneath the wide-spreading shelter

Of the royal wings, lasting peace
Will be established, Paradise

Return to Earth.

*

A fitting garden is prepared.
The steep hillside's blasted clear
For the terraces. No axis steers
Towards the old castle. Here

A new world's in the making.
All learning's to combine,
Lay open the Book of Nature,
Its paradisial proportions

And harmonies; parterres
In the shape of musical themes.
Melodies issuing from grottos,
Speaking statues, singing fountains,

(Water jets playing over
Hidden pipes). Technology
In service to a living cosmos
Restored in symbol, plant and tree,

In geometrical design, an eighth
Wonder of the World, (L-shaped);
The lowest terrace with its orange trees
About a central basin so designed

To be the gathering point for water
From every fountain in the garden.
A hillside dream the like of which
That when I waked I cried to dream again.

*

No dream.

Time's also of the essence here
In maze and sundial,
In the hastening seasons
Laid out in the Floral Calendar,

Or the Oval Staircase down which
Water slides in ever-widening ripples.

And all the magic
        Falls away as you
                Raise your gaze
                        To the garden's

Highest point on the upper terrace.
There, clad in armour, sword in hand
Eden's protector, the lord of all he sees,

Frederick
        frozen in stone.
                The new St George

Whose fateful garden manifesto
Will soon be blasted black along

With swathes of Europe
Condemned to death by the breath

Of the avenging Hapsburg dragon.

Meanwhile...

Outside the Garden, the parks
Of royal Eden? Woodlands,

Wastes, the nurseries of *rogues*
And vagabonds, footloose, masterless.

Infestations o*f fleas and lice,*
The idle poor and their thin cattle.

Vermin that will eat us up unless
We fence them out, show them

What's for their labouring good:
To be set to work for us.

To Whom Belongs the Land?

Once a King's head falls,
Once the Nation's delivered from civil war
And a Commonwealth is born?

To whom belongs the Land

Once the poor combine to dig, manure the Waste,
The Wilderness as yet in common
And labour no curse,

Only the hand which grasps to take and own?

To whom belongs the Land,

Its wealth a slumbering giant
To be roused by its sons and daughters
In collective cultivation for the general good?

The sun of Reason,
Of Love rising; hand-in-hand
With Christ indwelling to lift up

The creation from the bondage of the Fall.

To whom belongs the Land

Once the poor are freed
from crowns,
landlords,
meddling clerics,

And the World's turned upside-down?

No Limits

Reason, refined of its impurities
And unrestrained. Nature, buried
Beneath *a heap of jarring atoms.*

Whatever harmony, refinement,
Beauty is to be expressed here, lies
In the calculating mind of Man.

*

The garden as controlling intellect;
As foil for the display of power,
Reason's unerring rays a cold,

Joyless sun. Number, calculation
Lie like a heavy frost: two thousand
Four hundred and fifty six fountains

To be supplied; no obstacle too great
That Apollo's rays can't pierce
And Hercules' club subdue. It's a war

The army's called to wage. Thirty-six
Thousand souls perilously engaged;
Whether to suffer death by marsh gas

For the sake of the Grand Canal;
Or be one of ten thousand sacrificed
In three years of failure to build

The aqueduct to keep the fountains
On display. Looking along the central
Axis, human figures dwindle to pinheads

Dotted about the avenue as it recedes
From sight. This is Eden as imagined
By the Snake. No limits to its glory;

(Nor to its withering blight).

Cogito Ergo Sum

I think therefore I am

The Book of Nature's torn in two
And buried with its broken wand
Deeper than did ever plummet sound.

And Jacob's Ladder's followed on,
Collapsed into the gaping ground
As too the Rainbow Bridge, dissolved

Into the blue.

The Wealth of Nations

*If you should destroy these vessels, yet our principles
you can never extinguish but they will live forever
and enter into other bodies to live and speak and act.
(Edward Burroughs to the Restoration Government)*

A Parting Blast

Wealth streams to Britain's shores,
Periphery to centre. It means
Winners and losers. One's sovereignty
At risk from another's use of force.
Labour enslaved, whether shipped

From Africa or hired from the commons
Of the landless poor. The Second Coming
Has not come. Love, Reason, Christ
Rising in us to collective self-reliance.
World-wide trade's the grander option,

That we may the better set forth and show
The pride of our hearts in decking our proud
Carcasses and feeding our greedy guts
With superfluous unnecessary curiosities.
(A parting blast from one unreconciled).

Unfrozen?

Expanding commerce, rising wealth
Percolate the country-wide estates.
Nature, unfrozen from Mind's

Deep freeze, is placed in warm-
Lit frames of Arcadian scenes
Or the Picturesque. Geometry's rule

Has given way to the softly contoured
Landscape park, the serpentine lake,
The stands of stately trees. Nature's

Freed (and now needs much
More room in which to breathe).

A Small Matter

A drawing made in July 1721

Shock jolts the sleepy countryside.
It's the small matter of a new wooden fence
Staked across an open field farmed
In common for more years
Than memory can trace. Abrupt.

A wordless statement of intent
That the Squire's garden is to be
(Considerably) enlarged. Still visible
Through the growing lawn the strips
Ploughed ready to be sown, continue

To the former garden wall; like
The high-water mark of a retreating sea
That once served to define and hold
In place the Squire's boundaries.

Prospect Painting c1710

'Nor fence of ownership crept in between
To hide the prospect from the following eye'
                                        John Clare

Push aside your curtains. Look out
Over the countryside. There's
The Meadows, common land
A mile broad; expanses of open fields
As far as the eye can see, green

And featureless though just below
Your window the fields are ridged
And furrowed for sowing. There are
A few trees but your eyes are drawn
To rest upon the natural boundaries:

The broad course of the river, the hills
On the horizon, the pathless distances
In between. You gaze and dream.
Two roads, barely visible, their course
Marked out with trees, meet to cross

A bridge over the river. There's a tiny
Church tower in the distance rising
Out of the enveloping green. This
Is a sleepy world whose picture
(Painted by commission) is proof

That somewhere, someone's waking up.

Half-Clothed

from a drawing of 1721

From this rising ground, the Estate
Appears but half-clothed in the trees
Of its newly planted woodland park.

Who now is left the more exposed?

Those in the Great House as yet wide-
Open to the north, or those reliant
On the remaining furlong strips whose

Ancient rights still extend to nudge
Their Lordship's naked boundary wall
In common sight of one and all?

Old England

Landscape Watercolour c1813

Commoners, gleaners, bent
To their tasks in the boundless fields,
Some taking their ease
In the shade of stooks.

Below, the plain spreads
Featureless save for threads of trees,
Glint of a river;
A land asleep

And these free to dream;
Bound to the earth yet living in
Such distances,
The faint line

Of the purple hills on the horizon.
Some, high on the loaded wagons,
Stand, tiny figures,
Against the changeless circle

Of earth and sky.

Classical Landscape Garden

Mid 18th Century

Nature framed in art. A dream-past
Summoned into a tranquil space of trees
Mirrrored in acres of lake, in temples

Of serenity. Apollo's on the hill
Overlooking folly-ruins of sweet neglect,
Grottos to mimic elemental force held

Back at the fence and admitted only
To refine, uplift and please. Nature
Enhanced to new standards of good taste

(Bourne on ruthless seas of rising wealth).

The Wealth of Nations

The Enlightenment's put in at Kingston, Jamaica.
A steamer trunk of books for Thomas Thistlewood
Of Lincolnshire. Plantation owner, avid reader,
Student of Adam Smith. He understands (better

Than the Scot?) what it takes to source prosperity,
Advance the new world order. Free labour helps.
And being outnumbered twenty to one, his rule
Of terror, if not enlightened is nothing if not

Rational. He studies. How best to wound
Without losing the next day's labour? So opens
Ruts in the flesh just deep enough to make
The most of pepper, lime, salt, his concocted

Mixture to be rubbed into the wound to work
Its finely calculated agony. Flogging perfected.
And nothing personal. Just one in a range
Of strategies to keep the business viable.

His diaries note the sexual favours he enjoys,
Mingling with those he considers innately
Predisposed to savagery. Thomas Thistlewood
Shouldering the White Man's Burden

And prospering against all the odds.

Look to the Land

The Law doth punish man or woman
That steals the goose from off the common
But lets the greater felon loose
That steals the common from the goose.

The House

from a view painted c 1760

It appears set back, (ancestral woods
To the rear) as if it were itself
The springhead giving out
To the wider countryside its sense

Of *verdant plenty*, of settled peace,
The river winding placidly between
The fields (open as yet), the meadows
Still in common and safe (surely)

Within the benign manorial reach.

from a view drawn in 1721

The same scene. The same
Three-gabled mansion, now
At the heart of an ancient village.

Twelve cottages, church,
Vicarage, mill. All, saving
The church, to be demolished

For the emparkment of the Hall:
The new sensibility required
Of Lord and landed class;

The extended boundaries
Necessary to best express
The new refinement, wealth's

Excess and power for
Improvement of the general good.
(Within the next sixty years all

Local commons will be enclosed.
Open field, meadow, wood).

Lament for a Way of Life Destroyed

a painting of 1812

Your needs required no softly contoured slopes
And scenic lakes. But the open fields for hay
And crops; common grazing for your animals;
Rights to gather wood, reeds, heather, bracken;
Woodland and hedgerow for forage; furze
To fire your bread oven, turbage for peat

Or turf for smoking your bacon. And time:
For work; for resting on your spade, for napping
In the shade or flirting with the milkmaid
Under the old oak. There you are on the heath
With your dog and sheep, the epitome
Of *independent life*, praised as the frame

Of freedom by the poet. Bane of the Improvers,
You were one of those able to *bask all day*
In the sun rather than fall in line: waged,
Productive, head bent to the plough at dawn
Tearing up the commons for *a harvest*
Which the rich shall reap. You stand looking out

At us as your dog looks up at you, the master.
One *who has no communication with and therefore*
No reverence for the opinion of the world. Quite so.
Your views were never sought. *The paths stopt…*
Stolen from the trampled poor. And so much more;
Scorn for the income a cottager could earn

From grazing geese: *beggarly* when viewed
From one's landscaped lawn. You're standing
On the heath, free (as yet) to choose which path
To roam. But Nature's good for trade
And money's being made to talk. It *supersedes*
All else. Your rough and ready Eden was

A commodity far too good
                    To be left to the likes of you.

First Fruits

To the ruling class assembled,
The unholy Dove descends.
Cold flames rest on every head;
First fruits of Thinking Man

As world-wide trade expands
Into the new mysteries
Of the market place and
The Invisible Hand. Mary's

Present, too: become Nature
Administering misery
To the landless poor: Her
Bitter medicine's *the unassisted*

Operation of principles for a future cure.
Blake's outrage. Clare's lament
At a lost content as land turns
To gold and money *supersedes all else.*

Unholy Pentecost

The rushing mighty wind fills
The entire House with Enclosure Bills.
Improvement rests on every head.
What's held in common needs
Dividing up, large farms to swallow

The small. The Cottager's left with
No rights at all, shorn of pasture, fuel.
Game Laws, Trespass, Laws
Of Settlement confine you
To your degraded spot. Labour

Is all you've left to give. The creditor
Takes your cow and pig. Ploughed up,
Fenced off, the old ways of sufficiency;
The rough edge of wages take their place
Ever to lag behind the price of wheat.

Profits will be protected and increase
While you'll apply for Poor Relief
Bound over into a lifetime's slavery
Of degrading want. Your varied diet's
As lost a luxury as the land under your feet.

To combine's against the Law. To join
And agitate for more creates a mob.
You may be hanged or find your way
In chains to the transportation hulks
Although you've shed no blood.

The workhouse, abhorred, begrudged
Is what remains of hope and comfort
To your old age. That, and to be taught
Your consolation in the final proportions
Of eternal justice according to *Burke's*

Unholy Dove.

A Sorry Tale

of dispossession

Last bolt-hole of paradise,
If only an allotment saved
From commercial smothering.
As for a house, a garden

And the magic means
That gives one leave to own,
Thereby lurks a sorry tale
Of public-private theft,

Land disappeared from under
The Commons' feet,
The profits pocketed.
Labour, landless, let loose

To earn its lawful access
To what its Betters hold
Fenced off in legal stock;
Imagine! A World where

The *Rights* all hold *self-evident*
To Life, to Liberty, to Happiness,
Do not extend an open hand
To shares in the common

Wealth of Land!

Nature

Natura naturans

Ground into a wonderland of atomic dust,
Now waves, now particles whirling in and out
Of space and time; sublime quantum paradise

Glimpsed through an ever-enlarging lens
So fine only the few can understand; Nature
Is this truly You, the whole of You that I
Now see as I look out into the heights of June:

The grasses flowering, hollyhocks eight feet tall,
Bright hawkweeds, roses red, yellow, pink
Unfolding speech beyond the soulless song
And dance of their atomic whirl? Speech

That speaks of an all-embracing warmth;
Of joy, of love; of *your maternal life*, Nature,
Which, as gift, *I bear within the essence of my will.*

Three Poems for Anne Marie

1

The Homestead

Well over twenty years ago
Our cottage garden was rank grass
Where a few vegetables had grown,

Divided from the farmer's grazing
By a mixed hedge and shaded
With leylandi. He added

Half an acre into the bargain,
Wide views open to the west
And the neighbouring hills.

Later, we bought two more acres,
So the cottage with its abandoned
Hilltop garden turned (returned?)

Into a homestead such as a Cottager,
Living in this neighbourhood three
Centuries ago, might have enjoyed

When all was the Waste and rights
To common land and a roof over
Your head was still the ancient way.

No idyll, of course. But at what cost
Improvement, once the thought took hold
That Nature has no soul and land's

To be viewed as money in the bank,
A private asset best hoarded
                    until the price is right?

                    *

What is wealth? Who are the poor?
What confines? What restlessness
Drives us to an unfamiliar shore?

Alpine forest, stream and rock.
Sweet pasture on your doorstep; hayloft,
Milking parlour, pig-pen, woodstore,

Integral to your house. Then- this
Invisible Hand, spread over the world,
Rails and highways the gripping fingers

Of its advance. As you're growing up
It's laying hold of your mountain side,
Its idling pastures, turning them

Into tourist flats, cars rather than sheep
And cows in need of stabling. All manner
Of services are following in its wake.

You'll feel impelled to leave. We'll meet,
In this far country which has no trees
(According to your mother). Wicker

Suitcase in hand, (cowbell to follow later),
You'll step ashore, finances in rude health
In exchange for your share of your family's

Outdated peasant wealth.

2

The Smallholding

A fair exchange

Every morning now
You leave the warmth
Of my side, leaving me

The night's gift of your warmth
To blanket me for a few
Sleepy minutes more: always

The first to greet the dog,
Turn the key in the door,
Bucket in hand and step

Out of night into day:
Into breathing light
Or lingering gloom,

Into driving wind and rain
Or the basking calm
Of a summer's dawn: always

Your steps the first to be
Imprinted in dew or frost
On the lawn. Now

You are climbing the stile,
Now crouching, tucked in close,
Washing the udder. Now

The warm milk is frothing
In the pail. Every morning
This exchange: our warmth

For that warm breathing hollow;
The two of them, cow and calf
Shifting in the straw,

Quietly disposing of the hay;
Wide eyes closed down
Gazing into the Far-Away.

Every morning this exchange
Of warmth for warmth; of tended
Pasture for a flow of milk.

3

The Garden

Inner aspect

The warmth of being so enclosed with flowers,
Sheltered by hazel… The trim lawn
As breathing space. At the far end tiered
Branches of magnolia frame a metal bench
Set in a shady wilderness of fern, euphorbia.

Hostas overlook the pond from their gravel bed
And a star-cluster of lilies leaning from their pot,
Broadcast the full force of their summer fragrance
As you pass. A dragonfly takes wing from reeds
Beside the pond whose raft of lily pads stretches

Side to side, each large enough to float a frog
Were one to venture from the shelter of the rocks.
Over years, the path surround has been defined
With a carpet of creeping thyme now
In purple bloom. In every crevice pioneers

Are looking for fresh ground. Ferns unfurl
From darknesses of wood and rock. Holly,
First in the greenwood, looks to settle among
The flowers or (given leave) finds root-room
In the decay of an old damson stump.

It's a work to keep up: and we're part of it
Not set apart; balancing wilderness, planting
And design: the rockery once scooped out
To make the pond, the stumps where ivy
Scrambles, all that remain of leylandi

Which once shut out the sun. At length
A garden comes into its own: the kingdoms
Responding to our paths and borderlines,
The elements in constant play; winged ones
Feeding, bathing, raising young; hedgehog

Snuffling in the undergrowth or making
Moonlit haste across the lawn; fullness
Of growth, of ripening and decline;
Our faults of ignorance, inattention
Or neglect. But in the end, for all this work,

For all our love, to know the warmth
Of being so blessed with flowers, sheltered
By hazel, watched over by the waving trees…

Outer Aspect

Step through the arch of climbing roses
And the countryside pours in: hilltop views
Expanding west to wooded hills
And the treeless line of the Black Mountains.

Breathe in the summer sky, a sea of island clouds
Shape-shifting, drifting by. What's to come?

This hilltop was once the Waste, then pasture;
Now, this patch has turned part lawn, the rest
Tilled and planted. Fruit trees, fruit bushes,
Herbs and flowers and vegetables all in rows.

Extraordinary these arising forms; intimacy
Of seed and soil; of warmth and weather,
Working fingers, the due processes of time,
Heaped-up waste and kitchen scraps inviting

The freely-gifted labour of the World's wisdom,
And awaiting their return to earth and all
The myriad lives, the invisible threads inwoven
That create the living spirit of a place. This

Half acre we've awoken over years to bounty,
Beauty, isn't this what it means to live in wealth?
Nurturing Nature evoking loving work- and far
Beyond the confines of a private garden patch?

Breathe in the summer sky, a sea of island clouds
Shape-shifting drifting by. What's to come?

Look to the Land

Properly understood, the laws that govern
the production and distribution of wealth
show that the want and injustice of the
present social state are not necessary.
                    Henry George 1879

In danger to be removed like a cottage. Or have
One's home repossessed or be forced
Onto the streets by the rising rent, one

More family moving bags and suitcases
From one lodging to the next,
While second homes stand vacant

As their ocean views and apartments
With gold fittings within walking distance
Of pavement squats are readied

To refresh the occasional landings of jet-
Lagged Owners on Progress from one
Mansion to the next. To ask what

Negates a just social order founded
On love of neighbour and equal rights,
Look to the Land: how it's possessed,

By whom and who's extracting rent.
For those with few means are still *despised*
And cannot have justice (as complained

John Bunyan's wife). They live *in danger*
To be removed like a cottage. (Or, in spite
Of warnings, of burning to death

In their ill-clad tower block.)

And did those Feet?

Blake's 'Jerusalem'

It's the question, the mere suggestion
That sparks the mental fight, (the poor
Being driven out of Eden, like beasts
Harnassed to the profit plough).

And now, as stirring anthem, it mingles
In the nation's pride, even as it casts
Into relief the fall of Albion into line:
The steel rails of Progress laid

To the drum-beat of Necessity,
An underworld of *satanic* force
Powering mill and mine and factory.
The question, the mere suggestion

Of *those feet*, that *Countenance divine*,
Is all that's needed for Imagination
To summon every mental weapon
To its aid, raise *Jerusalem's* foundations

In the questing mind, the burning heart.

Blessed Continuance?

Site Visit

We're a dozen, crowding into one barn after another.
Straw-strewn, muddy, dark. But comforting,
The sense of something familiar and close
To the heart; the warm breath of animals,
The busy working cries of men, the restless
Shifting of horses' hooves in the straw, their ring
In the light on the courtyard stones outside...

The years crowd around us. We guess
At the lofty spaces over our heads. Daylight
Angles its rays through gaps in the slates;
One doorless threshold leads to another:
Feeding troughs, rusting machinery,
A few steps up to a different level. Gaps
In the floor. Creaking stairs winding
To a loft, a children's paradise...

We explore. More darkness. An iron
Water tank fills up in a dim recess,
Trickling water the sole sound of life.
The floor's littered with droppings,
A swallow's nest tucked into the rafters.
Corners too dark to assess. A hush. Then
'The nursery could be here' someone says.

Returning to the courtyard, we gather
In the brisk air of the winter evening,
Midsummer shining in midwinter's dark.

These abandoned chambers that once
Provided food, we with good will
And the manifested means could turn
Again into busy places of nourishment,

The dying farm become a thriving school...

The Picnic

an incident
from the twenty-first century

*'What would you think if I
Were to picnic on your lawn?'*

Thus the lady of the manor, dismounted
And I with my class of nine-year-olds
Caught bums on the grass on
The literal verge of wrong a few
Feet from the public path, green acres
Stretching to wooded hills beyond,
Tell-tale sandwiches and flasks in hand.

Her dogs were wagging merrily, oblivious
To territorial outrage and the deference
Due to one owning so many manorial acres,
This the sorest of sore points:
That I failed to rise and apologise.
(But then I didn't realise the grievous
Nature of my fault nor who she was).

A contrite letter was required
And so the matter closed.

*

Manners? Grace? Tact? No quarter given
For the offender to save face
Beneath the gaze of his watching class,
But a class lesson in the power
Of ownership to put you in your place

Played out on lawns once common land,
The site of peasant dwellings
Encroached upon through lordly power,
Not the exercise of gentle hands
Nor gracious manners;

Powers to fence the Commons off
From landed shares in the common-wealth;
(Indeed how else could we have progressed
To lead the World in Industry, Empire,
Still be so bedevilled by seismic splits of class?)

Yet still to cherish stately homes as if they
Were our own, the wealth of landscaped parks,
The romance of influence in high places
All the heart could wish for!
But when the lady of the manor says

(In the manner of the Lady)

What would you think if I
Were to picnic on your lawn?...

Lower Mill Farm

What is this but the Spirit of England that calls?.
The spirit that dwells within the land...in its air...
its valleys, its fields, in its waters and in its trees.
                                                    (Joseph Conrad)

A leat once channelled water here across the fields
To power a grist mill. No trace of its course remains,
Nor of the mill wheel save the square housing
For the shaft and the buttressed wall. But the stream's
Sounding as ever in its slow-forming course, winter-
Swollen, and the abandoned buildings, farmhouse,
Barns all in a row, still rise high on the southern slope
(Brambles mounting to block windows in the lower walls
To the rear). Trees shadow the winding length
Of the stream and as you continue past the buildings
Following the pathless right of way, a facing hill
Answering your descending slope mounts steeply
To the skyline, sheep dotted along its spine-

While perched across fields rising to the west,
The village church, set there since medieval times,
Its sanctuary glimpsed end-on, the pointed statement
Of its modest spire blending into the view. You feel
Cradled here in such secluded wealth of pasture, trees,
The constant music of the stream, the gentle contours

Of the land, the old orchard, even the grey logs piled
Ready for use. And the buildings, (the church included)
Absent-present, their slumbering power to reawaken
Abundance. Well-being's in the air. Welcome.
A breathing stillness as though some Beauty were sleeping
That could be kissed awake, raised up by the embrace
Of true lovers, warriors of peace with new ways
And means of restoring land to the community,
Reawakening its common wealth as never before.

And in perpetuity.

Sleeping Beauty

Suddenly, everything comes to a halt.
The Land falls into disuse, the Office Block
Turns into a wilderness of weeds, litter,
Crushed cans, shards of window glass.

The People look on, wish the Block
Demolished, the Land returned to use.
Fourteen years pass by. Restive, they
Prepare a Compulsory Purchase Order

And out of the Law rides a thousand years
Of Private Property; at stake the absent
Owner's human rights. Once more
The People are repulsed and Beauty,

Tucked up amidst the mounting rubbish
Sleeps on spellbound until such time
As she'll be kissed to death, transformed
From Land into figures in her Owner's

Swelling bank account.

Common Wealth

Adam Smith's 'The Wealth of Nations'

I am come to bind [Nature] *to your service*
and make her your slave. Francis Bacon (1602)

And was Jerusalem builded here
Among these dark satanic mills?
W. Blake: Jerusalem (1804)

*

The Slave Trade's banned as Nature's bound,
To yield the stuff Empires are made of,
Her inmost parts mechanised and set
To work wonders; (wealth for a few
Prosperity for some, World Wars
For everyone).
          Adam Smith, beloved
For warmth of heart, friendship,
Generosity, looks on: *impartial spectator*

As if all the facts were known:

The natural progress of liberty: trust,
Mutual regard, commercial peace
And equity, set trembling in the scales

Against *the prodigal, the spirit of system,*
Conspiracies to cheat, deceive, *the love*
Of domination and authority over others.

                As if all the facts were known:

Aysmmetries of power, information;
The singular commercial mind *contracted*
And rendered incapable of elevation, traffic
Made of the poor and every lower instinct.

Yet that precious need of one for another
In freedom of exchange; the drive
To better ourselves, uncover the virtue
Of who we are:
                    to love and be lovely;

And always willing the sacrifice of private
Gain, if contrary to a general good.

                As if all the facts were known...

And still the trembling scales were to hold,
For convergence of awakened hearts
To weigh the balance, win release

To mingle freely with the gods and spirits
Of the dead in the fields of Aalu:

Commerce become one worldwide blessing
Of Nature freed from slavery, and ourselves
Restored to union
         with the sacredness of the World.

Notes on the poems

Ancient Egypt: Hapi: god of the Inundation of the Nile

Ancient Greece: the words in italics are from 'Spring' by Meleager of Gadara, first century BC

Ancient Rome: The Death of Pan told in Plutarch's *Moral Essays*

The Garden Sepulchre: 'At the place where he had been crucified there was a garden and in this garden a new tomb in which no-one had yet been buried.' (John, chp 19)

Legendary Magnificence: Ladon's hundred heads. Serpent-like monster twined around the tree in the Garden of the Hesperides, guarding the golden apples.

World Wonder: 'That when I waked...' Caliban, The Tempest

Meanwhile: 'The poor increase like fleas and lice and these vermin will eat us up unless we enclose' (1665) quoted in Christopher Hill's *The World Turned Upside Down. (Penguin 1991)*

No Limits: a heap of jarring atoms: Dryden, A Song for St Cecilia's Day, 1687

Cogito Ergo Sum: Descartes, Discourse on Method, 1637; *Deeper than did ever plummet sound:* Prospero, The Tempest

*A Parting Blast: That we may the better set forth...*from Tyranipocrit Discovered 1649, quoted by Hill, p 337

A Small Matter: the drawings referred to here and elsewhere are taken from *Common Land in English Painting 1700-1850: Ian Waites (Boydell and Brewer 2012)*

The Wealth of Nations: see *Twilight of the Money Gods: John Rapley (Simon and Schuster 2017 pp 40-42)*

*Lament...independent life...*see James Thomson: *Liberty Part V, 1736:*
By these three virtues be the frame sustained/Of British freedom- independent life;/Integrity in office; and o'er all/ Supreme, a passion for the commonweal...

For what the people were able to achieve with the help of the common, see George Sturt's *Change in the Village* 1912: *With the common...they could, and did, achieve all this (*ie the 'independent life' referred to by Thomson). *I am not dealing in superstition. I have mentioned nothing here that I have not learnt from men who remember the system still flourishing.* (quoted in Waites, p 48)

For the various quotes in this poem, see Waites chp 5. For example: *The Splendid Village: Ebenezer Elliott, 1833: the footpaths stolen from the trampled poor…And common sown with curses loud and deep/Proclaim a harvest which the rich shall reap.*

or landscape designer Humphrey Repton in *Concerning Improvements* noted: *.the common is enclosed and the proprietor boasts, not that it produces corn for man or grass for cattle, but that it produces him rent: thus money supersedes every other consideration.* (Waites pp 104-5)

Unholy Pentecost: for background reading see *The Village Labourer 1760-1832 JL Hammond and Barbara Hammond,* first published by Longmans, Green and Co, London, 1911.

Burke's Unholy Dove: *Reflections on the Revolution in France,* quoted in the 1995 edition of the Village Labourer (Alan Sutton Publishing Limited by arrangement with Longman Group Limited, p 208): *The body of the people…must respect that property of which they cannot partake. They must labour to obtain what by labour can be obtained; and when they find, as they commonly do, the success disproportioned to the endeavour, they must be taught their consolation in the final proportions of eternal justice.*

A Sorry Tale: See the American Declaration of Independence 1776: *We hold these truths to be self-evident, that all men are created equal, that they are endowed by their Creator with certain inalienable Rights, that among these are Life, Liberty and the pursuit of Happiness…*

Nature: Natura naturans. The invisible being of Nature, as spiritual subject as distinct from *Natura naturata*, Nature as physical object ('one more fountain feature…') See *Gardening as a Sacred Art:* Jeremy Naydler (Floris Books 2011 p. 94)

your maternal life.: from the Michaelmas Meditation of Rudolf Steiner's Soul Calendar (1918)(translation by Ruth and Hans Pusch, Anthroposophic Press, 1988)

Look to the Land: In danger to be removed like a cottage: proverbial for the likes of John Bunyan. His parents had been cottagers. In 1661 his wife described him as a *tinker and a poor man therefore he is despised and cannot have justice. Quoted by Hill*

The Wealth of Nations: to mingle freely… Osiris: declaring a positive judgement, from: the Weighing of the Soul (The Egyptian Book of the Dead); other *italics* within the poem are the words of Adam Smith as quoted by Jesse Norman in *Adam Smith: What He Thought and Why it Matters (Allen Lane, 2018)*

Acknowledgements

Firstly, to Anne-Marie, my wife, for her constant support and patience in rising to the challenges of 'living with a poet' as she says.

Then, to all the sources of study detailed in the Notes, in particular, to Jeremy Naydler's 'Gardening as a Sacred Art' which first suggested the germ of a possible sequence;

the enlightening art work in Ian Waites' 'Common Land in English Painting, 1700-1850' which provided not only factual but visual inspiration;

the powerfully living resources captured in Christopher Hill's 'The World Turned Upside Down' and JL and B Hammonds' 'The Village Labourer, 1760-1832';

the recent study by Jesse Norman which opened my eyes to the as yet unrealised potential of the insights of Adam Smith;

and above all, for the constant, 'inwoven' inspiration of the seminal work of Rudolf Steiner, whose life and tireless activity in the first quarter of the twentieth century has sown the seeds for new directions in so many spheres of human life and provided pathways towards an evolutionary future for humanity which is full of hope.